Steps Towards a Small Theory of the Visible

John Berger

1926–2017

John Berger

Steps Towards a Small Theory of the Visible

PENGUIN BOOKS — GREAT IDEAS

PENGUIN BOOKS

UK | USA | Canada | Ireland | Australia
India | New Zealand | South Africa

Penguin Books is part of the Penguin Random House group
of companies whose addresses can be found at
global.penguinrandomhouse.com.

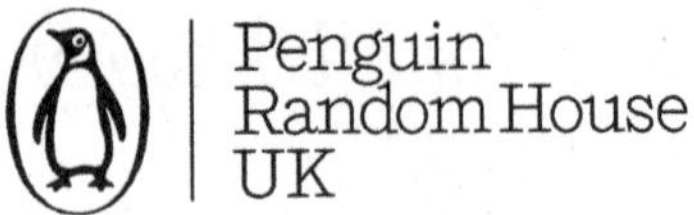

This selection published in Penguin Books 2020
004

Set in 12/15 pt Dante MT Std
Typeset by Jouve (UK), Milton Keynes
Printed and bound in Great Britain by Clays Ltd, Elcograf S.p.A.

A CIP catalogue record for this book
is available from the British Library

ISBN: 978-0-241-47287-3

www.greenpenguin.co.uk

Contents

Speech on Accepting the Booker Prize
for Fiction at the Café Royal in London
on 23 November 1972

Since you have awarded me this prize, you may like to know, briefly, what it means to me.

The competitiveness of prizes I find distasteful. And in the case of this prize the publication of the shortlist, the deliberately publicized suspense, the speculation on the writers concerned as though they were horses, the whole emphasis on winners and losers is false and out of place in the context of literature.

Nevertheless prizes act as a stimulus – not to writers themselves but to publishers, readers and booksellers. And so the basic cultural value of a prize depends upon what it is a stimulus to. To the conformity of the market and the consensus of average opinion; or to imaginative independence on the part of both reader and writer. If a prize only stimulates conformity, it merely underwrites success as it is conventionally understood. It constitutes no more than another chapter in a success story. If it stimulates imaginative independence, it encourages the will to seek alternatives. Or, to put it very simply, it encourages people to question.

The reason why the novel is so important is that the novel asks questions which no other literary form can ask: questions about the individual working on his own destiny; questions about the uses to which one can put a life – including one's own. And it poses these questions in a very private way. The novelist's voice functions like an inner voice.

Although it may seem somewhat inappropriate on my part, I would like to salute – and to thank – this year's jury for their independence and seriousness in this respect. All four books on their shortlist demonstrate the kind of imaginative non-conformity I'm talking about. That they gave a prize to my book gave me pleasure – because it represented a response, a response from other writers.

G took five years to write. Since then I have been planning the next five years of my life. I have begun a project about the migrant workers of Europe. I do not know what form the final book will take. Perhaps a novel. Perhaps a book that fits no category. What I do know is that I want some of the voices of the eleven million migrant workers in Europe and of the forty or so million that are their families, mostly left behind in towns and villages but dependent on the wages of the absent workers, to speak through and on the pages of this book. Poverty forces the migrants, year after year, to leave their own places and culture and come to do much of the dirtiest and worst-paid work in the industrialised areas of Europe, where they form the reserve army of labour. What is their view of the world? Of themselves? Of us? Of their own exploitation?

For this project it will be necessary to travel and stay in many places. I will need sometimes to take Turkish friends with me who speak Turkish, or Portuguese friends, or Greek. I want to work again with a photographer, Jean Mohr, with whom I made the book about the country doctor. Even if we live modestly as we ought to and travel in the cheapest way possible, the project of four years will cost about ten thousand pounds. I did not know exactly how we would find this money. I did not have any of it myself. Now the award of the Booker Prize would make it possible to begin.

Yet one does not have to be a novelist seeking very subtle connections to trace the five thousand pounds of this prize back to the economic activities from which they came. Booker McConnell have had extensive trading interests in the Caribbean for over 130 years. The modern poverty of the Caribbean is the direct result of this and similar exploitation. One of the consequences of this Caribbean poverty is that hundreds of thousands of West Indians have been forced to come to Britain as migrant workers. Thus my book about migrant workers would be financed from the profits made directly out of them or their relatives and ancestors.

More than that, however, is involved. The industrial revolution and the inventions and culture which accompanied it and which created modern Europe was initially financed by profits from the slave trade. And the fundamental nature of the relationship between Europe and the rest of the world, between black and white, has not changed. In G the statue of the four chained Moors is the most important single image of the book. This is why I have to turn this prize against itself. And I propose to do so by sharing it in a particular way. The half I give away will change the half I keep.

First let me make the logic of my position really clear. It is not a question of guilt or bad conscience. It certainly is not a question of philanthropy. It is not even, first and foremost, a question of politics. It is a question of my continuing development as a writer: the issue is between me and the culture which has formed me.

Before the slave trade began, before the European

de-humanised himself, before he clenched himself on his own violence, there must have been a moment when black and white approached each other with the amazement of potential equals. The moment passed. And henceforth the world was divided between potential slaves and potential slave-masters. And the European carried this mentality back to his own society. It became part of his way of seeing everything.

The novelist is concerned with the interaction between individual and historical destiny. The historical destiny of our time is becoming clear. The oppressed are breaking through the wall of silence which was built into their minds by their oppressors. And in their struggle against exploitation and neo-colonialism – but only through and by virtue of this common struggle – it is possible for the descendants of the slave and the slavemaster to approach each other again with the amazed hope of potential equals.

This is why I intend to share the prize with those West Indians in and from the Caribbean who are fighting to put an end to their exploitation. The London-based Black Panther movement has arisen out of the bones of what Booker and other companies have created in the Caribbean; I want to share this prize with the Black Panther movement because they resist both as black people and workers the further exploitation of the oppressed. And because, through their Black People's Information Centre, they have links with the struggle in Guyana, the seat of Booker McConnell's wealth, in Trinidad and throughout the Caribbean: the struggle whose aim is to expropriate all such enterprises.

You know as well as I do that the amount of money involved – as soon as one stops thinking of it as a literary prize – is extremely small. I badly need more money for my project about the migrant workers of Europe. The Black Panther movement badly needs money for their newspaper and for their other activities. But the sharing of the prize signifies that our aims are the same. And by that recognition a great deal is clarified. And in the end – as well as in the beginning – clarity is more important than money.

1972

Past Seen from a Possible Future

Has anyone ever tried to estimate how many framed oil paintings, dating from the fifteenth century to the nineteenth, there are in existence? During the last fifty years a large number must have been destroyed. How many were there in 1900? The figure itself is not important. But even to guess at it is to realize that what is normally counted as art, and on the evidence of which art historians and experts generalize about the European tradition, is a quantitatively insignificant fraction of what was actually produced.

From the walls of the long gallery, those who never had any reason to doubt their own significance look down in perpetual self-esteem, surrounded by gilded frames. I look down at the courtyard around which the galleries were built. In the centre, a fountain plays sluggishly: the water slowly but continuously overbrimming its bowl. There are weeping willows, benches and a few gesticulating statues. The courtyard is open to the public. In summer it is cooler than the city streets outside: in winter it is protected from the wind.

I have sat on a bench listening to the talk of those who come into the courtyard for a few minutes' break – mostly old people or women with children. I have watched the children playing. I have paced around the courtyard, when nobody was there, thinking about my own life. I have sat there, blind to everything around me, reading a newspaper. As I look down on the courtyard before turning back to the portraits of the nineteenth-century local dignitaries, I notice that the gallery attendant is standing at the next tall window and that he too is gazing down on the animated figures below.

And then suddenly I have a vision of him and me, each alone and stiff in his window, being seen from below. I am seen quite clearly but not in detail for it is forty feet up to the window and the sun is in such a position that it half dazzles the eyes of the seer. I see myself as seen. I experience a moment of familiar panic. Then I turn back to the framed images.

The banality of nineteenth-century official portraits is, of course, more complete than that of eighteenth-century landscapes or that of seventeenth-century religious pieces. But perhaps not to a degree that matters. European art is idealized by exaggerating the historical differences within its development and by never seeing it as a whole.

The art of any culture will show a wide differential of talent. But I doubt whether anywhere else the difference between the masterpieces and the average is as large as it is in the European tradition of the last five centuries. The difference is not only a question of skill and imagination, but also of morale. The average work – and increasingly after the sixteenth century – was produced cynically: that is to say its content, its message, the values it was nominally upholding, were less meaningful for the producer than the finishing of the commission. Hack work is not the result of clumsiness or provincialism: it is the result of the market making more insistent demands than the job.

Just as art history has concentrated upon a number of remarkable works and barely considered the largest part of the tradition, aesthetic theory has emphasized the disinterestedly spiritual experience to be gained from works of art and largely ignored their massive ideological function. We spiritualize art by calling it art.

The modern historians of Renaissance and post-Renaissance art – Burckhardt, Wölfflin, Riegl, Dvorak – began writing at the moment when the tradition was beginning to disintegrate. Undoubtedly the two facts were linked within a fantastically complicated matrix of other historical developments. Perhaps historians always require an end in order to begin. These historians, however, defined the various phases of the tradition (Renaissance, Mannerist, Baroque, Neo-Classic) so sharply and explained their evolution from one to the other with such skill that they encouraged the notion that the European tradition was one of change without end: the more it broke with or remade its own inheritance, the more it was itself. Tracing a certain continuity in the past they seemed to guarantee one for the future.

Concentration upon the exceptional works of a couple of hundred masters, an emphasis on the spirituality of art, a sense of belonging to a history without end – all these have discouraged us from ever seeing our pictorial tradition as a whole and have led us to imagine that our own experience of looking today at a few works from the past still offers an immediate clue to the function of the vast production of European art. We conclude that it was the destiny of Europe to make art. The formulation may be more sophisticated, but that is the essential assumption. Try now to see the tradition from the far distance.

'We can have no idea,' wrote Nietzsche, 'what sort of things are going to become history one day.

Perhaps the past is still largely undiscovered; it still needs so many retroactive forces for its discovery.'

During the period we are considering, which can be roughly marked out as the period between Van Eyck and Ingres, the framed easel picture, the oil painting, was the primary art product. Wall painting, sculpture, the graphic arts, tapestry, scenic design, and even many aspects of architecture were visualized and judged according to a value system which found its purest expression in the easel picture. For the ruling and middle classes the easel picture became a microcosm of the whole world that was virtually assimilable: its pictorial tradition became the vehicle for all visual ideals.

To what uses did the easel picture pre-eminently lend itself?

It permitted a style of painting which was able to 'imitate' nature or reality more closely than any other. What are usually termed stylistic changes – from classical to mannerist to baroque and so on never affected the basic 'imitative' faculty; each subsequent phase simply used it in a different manner.

I put inverted commas round 'imitative' because the word may confuse as much as it explains. To say that the European style imitated nature makes sense only when one accept a particular view of nature: a view which eventually found its most substantial expression in the philosophy of Descartes.

Descartes drew an absolute distinction between mind and matter. The property of mind was self-consciousness. The property of matter was extension in space. The mind was infinitely subtle. The workings of nature, however complicated, were mechanically explicable and, relative to the mind, unmysterious. Nature was predestined for man's use and was *the ideal object of his observation*. And it was precisely this which Renaissance perspective, according to which everything converged on the eye of the beholder, demonstrated. Nature was that conical segment of the visible whose apex was the human eye. Thus imitating nature meant tracing on a two-dimensional surface what that eye saw or might see at a given moment.

European art – I use the term to refer only to the period we are discussing – is no less artificial, no less arbitrary, no closer to total reality than the figurative art of any other culture or period. All traditions of figurative art invoke different experiences to confirm their own principles of figuration. No figurative works of art produced within a tradition appear unrealistic to those brought up within the tradition. And so we must ask a subtler question. What aspect of experience does the European style invoke? Or more exactly, what kind of experience do its means of representation represent? (Ask, too, the same question about Japanese art, or West African.)

In his book on the Florentine painters Berenson writes:

> It is only when we can take for granted the existence of the object painted that it can begin to give us pleasure that is genuinely artistic, as separated from the interest we feel in symbols.

He then goes on to explain that the tangibility, the 'tactile value' of the painted object, is what allows us to take its existence for granted. Nothing could be more explicit about the implications of the artistic pleasure to be derived from European art. That which we believe we can put our hands upon truly exists for us; if we cannot, it does not.

European means of representation refer to the experience of taking possession. Just as its perspective gathers all that is extended to render it to the individual eye, so its means of representation render all that is depicted into the hands of the individual owner-spectator. Painting becomes the metaphorical act of appropriation.

The social and economic modes of appropriation changed a great deal during the five centuries. In fifteenth-century painting the reference was often directly to what was depicted in the painting – marble floors, golden pillars, rich textiles, jewels, silverware. By the sixteenth century it was no longer assembled or hoarded riches which the painting rendered up to the spectator-owner but, thanks to the unity that chiaroscuro could give to the most dramatic actions, whole *scenes* complete with their events and protagonists. These scenes were 'own-able' to the degree that the spectator understood that wealth could produce and control action at a distance. In the eighteenth century the tradition divided into two streams. In one, simple middle-class properties were celebrated, in the other the aristocratic right to buy performances and to direct an unending theatre.

I am in front of a typical European nude. She is painted with extreme sensuous emphasis. Yet her sexuality is only superficially manifest in her actions or her own expression; in a comparable figure within other art traditions this would not be so. Why? Because for Europe ownership is primary. The painting's sexuality is manifest not in what it shows but in the owner-spectator's (mine in this case) right to see her naked. Her nakedness is not a function of her sexuality but of the sexuality of those who have access to the picture. In the majority of

European nudes there is a close parallel with the passivity which is endemic to prostitution.

It has been said that the European painting is like a window open on to the world. Purely optically this may be the case. But is it not as much like a safe, let into the wall, in which the visible has been deposited?

So far I have considered the methods of painting, the means of representation. Now to consider what the paintings showed, their subject matter. There were special categories of subjects: portraits, landscapes, still life, genre pictures of 'low life'. Each category might well be studied separately within the same general perspective which I have suggested. (Think of the tens of thousands of still-life canvases depicting game shot or bagged: the numerous genre pictures about procuring or accosting: the innumerable uniformed portraits of office.) I want, however, to concentrate on the category which was always considered the noblest and the most central to the tradition – paintings of religious or mythological subjects.

Certain basic Christian subjects occurred in art long before the rise of the easel painting. Yet described in frescoes or sculpture or stained glass their function and their social, as distinct from purely iconographic, meaning was very different. A fresco presents its subject within a given context – say that of a chapel devoted to a particular saint. The subject *applies* to what is structurally around it and to what is likely to happen around it; the spectator, who is also a worshipper, becomes part of that context. The easel picture is without a precise physical or emotional context because it is transportable.

Instead of presenting its subject within a larger whole it offers its subject to whoever owns it. Thus its subject *applies* to the life of its owner. A primitive transitional example of this principle working are the crucifixions or nativities in which those who commissioned the painting, the donors, are actually painted in standing at the foot of the cross or kneeling around the crib. Later, they did not need to be painted in because physical ownership of the painting guaranteed their immanent presence within it.

Yet how did hundreds of somewhat esoteric subjects apply to the lives of those who owned paintings of them? The sources of the subjects were not real events or rituals but texts. To a unique degree European art was a visual art deriving from literature. Familiarity with these texts or at least with their personae was the prerogative of the privileged minority. The majority of such paintings would have been readable as representational images but unreadable as language because they were ignorant of what they signified. In this respect if in no other most of us today are a little like that majority. What exactly happened to St Ursula? we ask. Exactly why did Andromeda find herself chained to the rocks?

This specialized knowledge of the privileged minority supplied them with a system of references by which to express subtly and evocatively the values and ideals of the life lived by their class. (For the last vestiges of this tradition note the moral value still sometimes ascribed to the study of the classics.) Religious and mythological paintings were something more than mere illustration of their separate subjects; together they constituted a system which classified and idealized reality according to the cultural interest of the ruling classes. They supplied a visual etiquette – a series of examples showing how significant moments in life should be envisaged. One needs to remember that, before the photograph or the cinema, painting alone offered recorded evidence of what people or events looked like or should look like.

Paintings applied to the lives of their spectator-owners because they showed how these lives should ideally appear at their heightened moments of religious faith, heroic action, sensuous abandon, contrition, tenderness, anger, courageous death, the dignified exercise of power, etc. They were like garments held out for the spectator-owners to put their arms into and wear. Hence the great attention paid to the verisimilitude of the *texture* of the things portrayed.

The spectator-owners did not identify themselves with the subjects of the paintings. Empathy occurs at a simpler and more spontaneous level of appreciation. The subjects did not even confront the spectator-owners as an exterior force; they were already theirs. Instead, the spectator-owners identified themselves *in* the subject. They saw themselves or their imagined selves covered over by the subject's idealized appearances. They found in them the guise of what they believed to be their own humanity.

The typical religious or mythological painting from the sixteenth century to the nineteenth was extraordinarily vacuous. We only fail to see this because we are deceived by the cultural overlay that art history has given these pictures. In the typical painting the figures are only superficially related to their painted surroundings; they appear detachable from them: their faces are expressionless: their vast bodies are stereotyped and limp – limp even in action. This cannot be explained by the artist's clumsiness or lack of talent; primitive works, even of a low order of imagination, are infinitely more expressive. These paintings are vacuous because it was their function, as established by usage and tradition, to be empty. They needed to be empty. They were not meant to express or inspire; they were meant to clothe the systematic fantasies of their owners.

The easel picture lent itself by its means of representation to a metaphorical appropriation of the material world: by its iconography to the appropriation by a small privileged minority of all 'the human values' of Christianity and the classic world.

I see a rather undistinguished Dutch seventeenth-century self-portrait. Yet the look of the painter has a quality which is not uncommon in self-portraits. A look of probing amazement. A look which shows slight questioning of what it sees.

There have been paintings which have transcended the tradition to which they belong. These paintings pertain to a true humanity. They bear witness to their artists' intuitive awareness that life was larger than the available traditional means of representing it and that its dramas were more urgent than conventional iconography could now allow. The mistake is to confuse these exceptions with the norms of the tradition.

The tradition and its norms are worth studying, for in them we can find evidence such as exists nowhere else of the way that the European ruling classes saw the world and themselves. We can discover the typology of their fantasies. We can see life rearranged to frame their own image. And occasionally we can glimpse even in works that are not exceptional – usually in landscapes because they relate to experiences of solitude in which the imagination is less confined by social usage – a tentative vision of another kind of freedom, a freedom other than the right to appropriate.

In one sense every culture appropriates or tries to make the actual and possible world its own. In a somewhat different sense all men acquire experience for themselves. What distinguishes post-Renaissance European practice from that of any other culture is its transformation of everything which is acquired into a commodity; consequently, everything becomes exchangeable. Nothing is appropriated for its own sake. Every object and every value is transmutable into another – even into its opposite. In *Capital,* Marx quotes Christopher Columbus writing in 1503: 'By means of gold one can even get souls into Paradise.' Nothing exists in itself. This is the essential spiritual violence of European capitalism.

Ideally the easel picture is framed. The frame emphasizes that within its four edges the picture has established an enclosed, coherent and absolutely rigorous system of its own. The frame marks the frontier of the realm of an autonomous order. The demands of composition and of the picture's illusory but all-pervasive three-dimensional space constitute the rigid laws of this order. Into this order are fitted representations of real figures and objects.

All the imitative skill of the tradition is concentrated upon making these representations look as tangibly real as possible. Yet each part submits to an abstract and artificial order of the whole. (Formalist analyses of paintings and all the classic demonstrations of compositional rules prove the degree of this submission.) The parts look real but in fact they are ciphers. They are ciphers within a comprehensive yet invisible and closed system which nevertheless pretends to be open and natural.

Such is the tyranny exercised by the easel painting, and from it arises the fundamental criterion for judging between the typical and the exceptional within the European tradition. Does what is depicted insist upon the unique value of its original being or has it succumbed to the tyranny of the system?

Today visual images no longer serve as a source of private pleasure and confirmation for the European ruling classes; rather, they have become a vehicle for its power over others through the mass media and publicity. Yet it is false to draw a comparison between these recent commercial developments and the hallowed tradition of European art. Their references may be different: they may serve a different immediate purpose; but their determining principle is the same – a man is what he possesses.

Delacroix was, I think, the first painter to suspect some of what the tradition of the easel picture entailed. Later, other artists questioned the tradition and opposed it more violently. Cézanne quietly destroyed it from within. Significantly, the two most sustained and radical attempts to create an alternative tradition occurred in the 1920s in Russia and Mexico, countries where the European model had been arbitrarily imposed on their own indigenous art traditions.

To most young artists today it is axiomatic that the period of the easel picture is finished. In their works they try to establish new categories in terms of media, form and response. Yet the tradition dies hard and still exerts an enormous influence on our view of the past, our ideas about the role of the visual artist and our definition of civilization. Why has it taken so long to die?

Because the so-called Fine Arts, although they have found new materials and new means, have found no new social function to take the place of the easel picture's outdated one. It is beyond the power of artists alone to create a new social function for art. Such a new function will only be born of revolutionary social change. Then it may become possible for artists to work truly concretely and constructively with reality itself, to work with what men are really like rather than with a visual etiquette serving the interests of a privileged minority; then it may be that art will re-establish contact with what European art has always dismissed – with that which cannot be appropriated.

1970

Turner and the Barber's Shop

There has never been another painter like Turner. And this is because he combined in his work so many different elements. There is a strong argument for claiming that it is Turner, not Dickens or Wordsworth or Walter Scott or Constable or Landseer, who, in his genius, represents most fully the character of the British nineteenth century. And it may be this which explains the fact that Turner is the only important artist who both before and after his death in 1851 had a certain popular appeal in Britain. Until recently a wide public felt that somehow, mysteriously, dumbly (in the sense that his vision dismisses or precludes words), Turner was expressing something of the bedrock of their own varied experience.

Turner was born in 1775, the son of a backstreet barber in central London. His uncle was a butcher. The family lived a stone's throw from the Thames. During his life Turner travelled a great deal, but in most of his chosen themes water, coastlines, or river banks recur continually. During the last years of his life he lived – under the alias of Captain Booth, a retired sea captain – a little further down the river at Chelsea. During his middle years he lived at Hammersmith and Twickenham, both overlooking the Thames.

He was a child prodigy and by the age of nine he was already earning money by colouring engravings; at fourteen he entered the Royal Academy Schools. When he was eighteen he had his own studio, and shortly afterwards his father gave up his trade to become his son's studio assistant and factotum. The relation between father and son was obviously close. (The painter's mother died insane.)

It is impossible to know exactly what early visual experiences affected Turner's imagination. But there is a strong correspondence between some of the visual elements of a barber's shop and the elements of the painter's mature style, which should be noticed in passing without being used as a comprehensive explanation. Consider some of his later paintings and imagine, in the backstreet shop, water, froth, steam, gleaming metal, clouded mirrors, white bowls or basins in which soapy liquid is agitated by the barber's brush and detritus deposited. Consider the equivalence between his father's razor and the palette knife which, despite criticisms and current usage, Turner insisted upon using so extensively. More profoundly – at the level of childish phantasmagoria – picture the always possible combination, suggested by a barber's shop, of blood and water, water and blood. At the age of twenty Turner planned to paint a subject from the Apocalypse entitled: *The Water Turned to Blood*. He never painted it. But visually, by way of sunsets and fires, it became the subject of thousands of his later works and studies.

Many of Turner's earlier landscapes were more or less classical, referring back to Claude Lorrain, but influenced also by the first Dutch landscapists. The spirit of these works is curious. On the face of it, they are calm, 'sublime', or gently nostalgic. Eventually, however, one realizes that these landscapes have far more to do with art than nature, and that as art they are a form of pastiche. And in pastiche there is always a kind of restlessness or desperation.

Nature entered Turner's work – or rather his imagination – as violence. As early as 1802 he painted a storm raging round the jetty at Calais. Soon afterwards he painted another storm in the Alps. Then an avalanche. Until the 1830s the two aspects of his work, the apparently calm and the turbulent, existed side by side, but gradually the turbulence became more and more dominant. In the end violence was implicit in Turner's vision itself; it no longer depended upon the subject. For example, the painting entitled *Peace: Burial at Sea* is, in its own way, as violent as the painting of *The Snowstorm*. The former is like an image of a wound being cauterized.

The violence in Turner's paintings appears to be elemental: it is expressed by water, by wind, by fire. Sometimes it appears to be a quality which belongs just to the light. Writing about a late painting called *The Angel Standing in the Sun*, Turner spoke of light *devouring* the whole visible world. Yet I believe that the violence he found in nature only acted as a confirmation of something intrinsic to his own imaginative vision. I have already suggested how this vision may have been partly born from childhood experience. Later it would have been confirmed, not only by nature, but by human enterprise. Turner lived through the first apocalyptic phase of the British Industrial Revolution. Steam meant more than what filled a barber's shop. Vermilion meant furnaces as well as blood. Wind whistled through valves as well as over the Alps. The light which he thought of as devouring the whole visible world was very similar to the new productive energy which was challenging and destroying all previous ideas about wealth, distance, human labour, the city, nature, the will of God, children, time. It is a mistake to think of Turner as a virtuoso painter of natural effects – which was more or less how he was officially estimated until Ruskin interpreted his work more deeply.

The first half of the British nineteenth century was profoundly unreligious. This may have forced Turner to use nature symbolically. No other convincing or accessible system of symbolism made a deep moral appeal, but its moral sense could not be expressed directly. The *Burial at Sea* shows the burial of the painter, Sir David Wilkie, who was one of Turner's few friends. Its references are cosmic. But as a statement, is it essentially a protest or an acceptance? Do we take more account of the impossibly black sails or of the impossibly radiant city beyond? The questions raised by the painting are moral – hence, as in many of Turner's later works, its somewhat claustrophobic quality – but the answers given are all ambivalent. No wonder that what Turner admired in painting was the ability to cast doubt, to throw into mystery. Rembrandt, he said admiringly, 'threw a mysterious doubt over the meanest piece of common'.

From the outset of his career Turner was extremely ambitious in an undisguisedly competitive manner. He wanted to be recognized not only as the greatest painter of his country and time, but among the greatest of all time. He saw himself as the equal of Rembrandt and Watteau. He believed that he had outpainted Claude Lorrain. This competitiveness was accompanied by a marked tendency towards misanthropy and miserliness. He was excessively secretive about his working methods. He was a recluse in the sense that he lived apart from society by choice. His solitariness was not a by-product of neglect or lack of recognition. From an early age his career was a highly successful one. As his work became more original, it was criticized. Sometimes his solitary eccentricity was called madness; but he was never treated as being less than a great painter.

He wrote poetry on the themes of his paintings, he wrote and sometimes delivered lectures on art, in both cases using a grandiloquent but vapid language. In conversation he was taciturn and rough. If one says that he was a visionary, one must qualify it by emphasizing hardheaded empiricism. He preferred to live alone, but he saw to it that he succeeded in a highly competitive society. He had grandiose visions which achieved greatness when he painted them and were merely bombastic when he wrote about them, yet his most serious conscious attitude as an artist was pragmatic and almost artisanal: what drew him to a subject or a particular painting device was what he called its *practicability* – its capacity to yield a painting.

Turner's genius was of a new type which was called forth by the British 19th century, but more usually in the field of science or engineering or business. (Somewhat later the same type appeared as hero in the United States.) He had the ability to be highly successful, but success did not satisfy him. (He left a fortune of £140,000.) He felt himself to be alone in history. He had global visions which words were inadequate to express and which could only be presented under the pretext of a *practical* production. He visualized man as being dwarfed by immense forces over which he had no control but which nevertheless he had discovered. He was close to despair, and yet he was sustained by an extraordinary productive energy. (In his studio after his death there were 19,000 drawings and watercolours and several hundred oil paintings.)

Ruskin wrote that Turner's underlying theme was Death. I believe rather that it was solitude and violence and the impossibility of redemption. Most of his paintings are as if about the aftermath of crime. And what is so disturbing about them – what actually allows them to be seen as beautiful – is not the guilt but the global indifference that they record.

On a few notable occasions during his life Turner was able to express his visions through actual incidents which he witnessed. In October 1834, the

Houses of Parliament caught fire. Turner rushed to the scene, made furious sketches and produced the finished painting for the Royal Academy the following year. Several years later, when he was sixty-six years old, he was on a steamboat in a snow storm and afterwards painted the experience. Whenever a painting was based on a real event he emphasized, in the title or in his catalogue notes, that the work was the result of first-hand experience. It was as though he wished to prove that life – however remorselessly – confirmed his vision. The full title of *The Snowstorm* was *Snowstorm. Steamboat off a Harbour's Mouth Making Signals in Shallow Water, and going by the Lead. The Author was in this storm on the night the Ariel left Harwich.*

When a friend informed Turner that his mother had liked the snowstorm painting, Turner remarked: 'I did not paint it to be understood, but I wished to show what such a scene was like: I got sailors to lash me to the mast to observe it; I was lashed for four hours, and I did not expect to escape, but I felt bound to record it if I did. But no one had any business to like the picture.'

'But my mother went through just such a scene, and it brought it all back to her.'

'Is your mother a painter?'

'No.'

'Then she ought to have been thinking of something else.'

The question remains what made these works, likeable or not, so new, so different. Turner transcended the principle of traditional landscape: the principle that a landscape is something which unfolds before you. In *The Burning of the Houses of Parliament* the scene begins to extend beyond its formal edges. It begins to work its way round the spectator in an effort to outflank and surround him. In *The Snowstorm* the tendency has become fact. If one really allows one's eye to be absorbed into the forms and colours on the canvas, one begins to realize that, looking at it, one is in the centre of a maelstrom: there is no longer a near and a far. For example, the lurch into the distance is not, as one would expect, *into* the picture, but out of it towards the right-hand edge. It is a picture which precludes the outsider spectator.

Turner's physical courage must have been considerable. His courage as an artist before his own experience was perhaps even greater. His truthfulness to that experience was such that he destroyed the tradition to which he was so proud to belong. He stopped painting totalities. *The Snowstorm* is the total of everything which can be seen and grasped by the man tied to the mast of that ship. There is *nothing* outside it. This makes the idea of anyone liking it absurd.

Perhaps Turner did not think exactly in these terms. But he followed intuitively the logic of the situation. He was a man alone, surrounded by implacable and indifferent forces. It was no longer possible to believe that what he saw could ever be seen from the outside – even though this would have been a consolation. Parts could no longer be treated as wholes. There was either nothing or everything.

In a more practical sense he was aware of the importance of totality in his life's work. He became reluctant to sell his paintings. He wanted as many of his pictures as possible to be kept together, and he became obsessed by the idea of bequeathing them to the nation so that they could be exhibited as a whole. 'Keep them together,' he said. 'What is the use of them but together?' Why? Because only then might they conceivably bear obstinate witness to his experience for which, he believed, there was no precedent and no great hope of future understanding.

1972

The Eaters and the Eaten

'The consumer society', so often and widely discussed as if it were a relatively new phenomenon, is the logical outcome of economic and technological processes which began at least a hundred years ago. Consumerism is intrinsic to nineteenth-century bourgeois culture. Consumption fulfils a cultural as well as an economic need. The nature of this need becomes clearer if we look at the most direct and simple form of consumption: eating.

How does the bourgeois approach his food? If we isolate and define this specific approach we will be able to recognize it when it is far more widely diffused.

The question could become complex because of national and historical differences. The French bourgeois attitude to food is not the same as the English. A German mayor sits down to his dinner with a somewhat different attitude from a Greek mayor. A fashionable banquet in Rome is not quite the same as one in Copenhagen. Many of the eating habits and attitudes described in Trollope and Balzac are no longer to be found anywhere.

Nevertheless an overall view, an outline, emerges if one compares the bourgeois manner of eating with the one, within the same geographical areas, from which it is most distinct: the peasant manner of eating. Working-class eating habits have less tradition than those of the other two classes because they are far more vulnerable to fluctuations of the economy.

On a world scale, the distinction between bourgeois and peasant is closely related to the brute contrast between plenty and scarcity. This contrast amounts to a war. But, for our limited purpose now, the distinction is not between the hungry and the overfed, but between two traditional views of the value of food, the significance of the meal and the act of eating.

At the outset it is worth noting a conflict in the bourgeois view. On the one hand, meals have a regular and symbolic importance in the life of bourgeois. On the other hand, he considers that to discuss eating is frivolous. This article, for example, cannot by its nature be serious; and if it takes itself seriously, it is pretentious. Cookbooks are bestsellers and most newspapers have their food columns. But what they discuss is considered a mere embellishment and is (mostly) the domain of women. The bourgeois does not think of the act of eating as a fundamental one.

The principal regular meal. For the peasant this meal is usually at mid-day; for the bourgeois it is usually dinner in the evening. The practical reasons for this are so obvious that they need not be listed. What may be significant is that the peasant meal is in the middle of the day, surrounded by work. It is placed in the day's stomach. The bourgeois meal comes after the day's work and marks the transition between day and evening. It is closer to the day's head (if the day begins with getting to the feet) and to dreams.

At the peasant's table the relationship between implements, food and eaters is intimate, and a value is conferred on use and handling. Each person has his own knife which he may well take out of his pocket. The knife is worn, used for many purposes other than eating, and usefully sharp. Whenever possible the same plate is kept throughout the meal, and between dishes it is cleaned with bread which is eaten. Each eater takes his share of the food and drink which are placed before all. For example: he holds the bread to his body, cuts a piece of it towards himself, and puts the bread down for another. Likewise with cheese or sausage. Contiguity as between uses, users and foods is treated as natural. There is a minimum of division.

On the bourgeois table everything that can be is kept untouched and separate. Every dish has its own cutlery and plate. In general plates are not cleaned by eating – because eating and cleaning are distinct activities. Each eater (or a servant) holds the serving dish to allow another to serve himself. The meal is a series of discrete, untouched gifts.

To the peasant all food represents work accomplished. The work may or may not have been his own or that of his family, but if it isn't, the work represented is nevertheless directly exchangeable with his own work. Because food represents physical work, the eater's body already 'knows' the food it is going to eat. (The peasant's strong resistance to eating any 'foreign' food for the first time is partly because its origin in the work process is unknown.) He does not expect to be surprised by food – except, sometimes, by its quality. His food is familiar like his own body. Its action on his body is *continuous* with the previous action of the body (labour) on the food. He eats in the room in which the food is prepared and cooked.

To the bourgeois, food is not directly exchangeable with his own work or activities. (The quality attributable to home-grown vegetables becomes exceptional.) Food is a commodity he buys. Meals, even when cooked at home, are purchased through a cash exchange. The purchase is delivered in a special room: the domestic dining-room, or restaurant. This room has no other purpose. It always has at least two doors or ways of entry. One door connects with his own daily life; through it he has entered in order to be served with food. The second door connects the kitchen; through it the food is brought out and the waste is taken away. Thus, in the dining-room, food is abstracted from its own production and from the 'real' world of his daily activities. Behind the two doors lie secrets: secrets of recipes behind the kitchen door; professional or personal secrets, not to be discussed at table, behind the other.

Abstracted, framed, insulated, the eaters and what is eaten form an isolated moment. This moment has to create its own content out of the air. The content tends to be theatrical: the décor of the table with its silver, glass, linen, china, etc.; the lighting; the relative formality of dress; the careful seating arrangements whenever there are guests; the ritualistic etiquette of table manners; the formality of serving; the transformation of the table between each act (course); and, finally, the leaving of the theatre together for a more dispersed and informal setting.

To the peasant, food represents work done and therefore repose. The fruit of labour is not only the 'fruit' but also the time taken from work time, spent in eating the food. Feasts apart, he accepts at table the sedative effect of eating. The appetite, satisfied, is quietened.

To the bourgeois the drama of eating, far from

being reposeful, is a stimulus. The theatrical invitation of the scene often provokes family dramas at meal times. The scene of the typical oedipal drama is not, as logically it might be, the bedroom, but the dinner table. The dining-room is the place of assembly where the bourgeois family appears to itself in public guise, and where its conflicting interests and power struggles are pursued in a highly formalized manner. The ideal bourgeois drama, however, is entertainment. The use of the word 'entertain' meaning to invite guests is significant here. Yet entertainment always proposes its opposite: boredom. Boredom haunts the insulated dining-room. Hence the conscious emphasis placed on dinner talk, wit and conversation. But the spectre of boredom also characterizes the way of eating.

The bourgeois overeats. Especially meat. A psychosomatic explanation may be that his highly developed sense of competition compels him to protect himself with a source of energy – proteins. (Just as his children protect themselves from the emotional cold with sweets.) The cultural explanation, however, is as important. If the scale of the meal is *spectacular*, all the eaters share in its achievement, and boredom is less likely. The shared achievement is not, fundamentally, culinary. The achievement is that of wealth. What wealth has obtained from nature is an affidavit that overproduction and infinite increase are natural. The variety, the quantity, the waste of food prove the *naturalness* of wealth.

In the nineteenth century with partridge, mutton and porridge for breakfast (in England), and three meats and two fish for dinner, the quantities were net, the proof extracted from nature arithmetical. Today with modern means of transport and refrigeration, the accelerated pace of daily life and a different use of the 'servant' classes, the spectacular is achieved in another way. The most varied and exotic foods are acquired out of season, and the dishes come from all over the world. Canard à la Chinoise is placed beside Steak Tartare and Boeuf Bourguignon. The affidavit obtained is no longer just from nature concerning quantity. It is also from history to testify how wealth unites the world.

By using the vomitorium the Romans separated the palate from the stomach in the pursuit of 'pleasure'. The bourgeois separates the act of eating from the body so that it can become, first, a spectacular social claim. The significance of the act of eating asparagus is not: I am eating this with pleasure; but: we *can* eat this here and now. The typical bourgeois meal is for each eater a series of discrete gifts. Each gift should be a surprise. But the message in each gift is the same: *happy the world which feeds you.*

The distinction between the principal regular meal

and the celebration or feast is very clear for the peasant, and often blurred for the bourgeois. (Which is why some of what I have written above borders, for the bourgeois, on the feast.) For the peasant what he eats and how he eats daily are continuous with the rest of his life. The rhythm of this life is cyclic. The repetition of meals is similar to, and connected with, the repetition of the seasons. His diet is local and seasonal. And so the foods available, the methods of cooking them, the variations in his diet, mark recurring moments throughout a lifetime. To become bored with eating is to be bored with life. This happens, but only to people whose unhappiness is very pronounced. The feast, small or large, is made to mark a special recurring moment or an unrepeatable occasion.

The bourgeois feast usually has more of a social than temporal significance. It is less a notch in time than the fulfilling of a social desideratum.

The feast for the peasant, when once the occasion has been given, begins with food and drink. It does so because food and drink have been reserved or put aside, on account of their rarity or special quality, for just such an occasion. Any feast, even if it is impromptu, has been partly prepared for for years. A feast is the consuming of the surplus saved and produced over and above daily needs. Expressing and using up some of this surplus, the feast is a double celebration – of the occasion which gives rise to it, and of the surplus itself. Hence its slow tempo, its generosity and the active high spirits which accompany it.

The feast for the bourgeois is an additional expense. What distinguishes its food from that of an ordinary meal is the amount of money spent. The true celebration of a surplus is beyond him, because he can never have a surplus of money.

The purpose of these comparisons is not to idealize the peasant. Peasant attitudes are mostly, in the strict sense of the word, *conservative*. At least until recently, the physical reality of the peasant's conservatism has hindered his understanding of the political realities of the modern world. These realities were originally a bourgeois creation. The bourgeois once had, and still to some degree retains, a mastery of the world of his own making.

I have tried to outline by using comparisons two modes of acquisition, of possessing, through the act of eating. If one examines each point of comparison, it becomes clear that the peasant way of eating is centred on the act of eating itself and on the food eaten: it is centripetal and physical. Whereas the bourgeois way of eating is centred on fantasy, ritual and spectacle: it is centrifugal and cultural. The first can complete itself in satisfaction; the second is never complete and gives rise to an appetite which, in essence, is insatiable.

1976

The Suit and the Photograph

What did August Sander tell his sitters before he took their pictures? And how did he say it so that they all believed him in the same way?

They each look at the camera with the same expression in their eyes. Insofar as there are differences, these are the results of the sitter's experience and character – the priest has lived a different life from the paper-hanger; but to all of them Sander's camera represents the same thing.

Did he simply say that their photographs were going to be a recorded part of history? And did he refer to history in such a way that their vanity and shyness dropped away, so that they looked into the lens telling themselves, using a strange historical tense: *I looked like this.* We cannot know. We simply have to recognise the uniqueness of his work, which he planned with the overall title of 'Man of the 20th Century'.

His full aim was to find, around Cologne in the area in which he was born in 1876, archetypes to represent every possible type, social class, sub-class, job, vocation, privilege. He hoped to take, in all, 600 portraits. His project was cut short by Hitler's Third Reich.

His son Erich, a socialist and anti-Nazi, was sent to a concentration camp where he died. The father hid his archives in the countryside. What remains today is an extraordinary social and human document. No other photographer, taking portraits of his own countrymen, has ever been so translucently documentary.

Walter Benjamin wrote in 1931 about Sander's work:

> It was not as a scholar, advised by race theorists or social researchers, that the author [Sander] undertook his enormous task, but, in the publisher's words, 'as the result of immediate observation.' It is indeed unprejudiced observation, bold and at the same time delicate, very much in the spirit of Goethe's remark: 'There is a delicate form of the empirical which identifies itself so intimately with its object that it thereby becomes theory.' Accordingly it is quite proper that an observer like Döblin should light upon precisely the scientific aspects of this opus and point out:

'Just as there is a comparative anatomy which enables one to understand the nature and history of organs, so here the photographer has produced a comparative photography, thereby gaining a scientific standpoint which places him beyond the photographer of detail.' It would be lamentable if economic circumstances prevented the further publication of this extraordinary corpus . . . Sander's work is more than a picture book, it is an atlas of instruction.

In the inquiring spirit of Benjamin's remarks I want to examine Sander's well-known photograph of three young peasants on the road in the evening, going to a dance. There is as much descriptive information in this image as in pages by a descriptive master like Zola. Yet I only want to consider one thing: their suits.

The date is 1914. The three young men belong, at the very most, to the second generation who ever wore such suits in the European countryside. Twenty or thirty years earlier, such clothes did not exist at a price which peasants could afford. Among the young today, formal dark suits have become rare in the villages of at least western Europe. But for most of this century most peasants – and most workers – wore dark three-piece suits on ceremonial occasions, Sundays and fêtes.

When I go to a funeral in the village where I live, the men of my age and older are still wearing them. Of course there have been modifications of fashion: the width of trousers and lapels, the length of jackets change. Yet the physical character of the suit and its message does not change.

Let us first consider its physical character. Or, more precisely, its physical character when worn by village peasants. And to make generalisation more convincing, let us look at a second photograph of a village band.

Sander took this group portrait in 1913, yet it could well have been the band at the dance for which the three with their walking sticks are setting out along the road. Now make an experiment. Block out the faces of the band with a piece of paper, and consider only their clothed bodies.

By no stretch of the imagination can you believe that these bodies belong to the middle or ruling class. They might belong to workers, rather than peasants; but otherwise there is no doubt. Nor is the clue their hands – as it would be if you could touch them. Then why is their class so apparent?

Is it a question of fashion and the quality of the cloth of their suits? In real life such details would be telling. In a small black and white photograph they are not very evident. Yet the static photograph shows, perhaps more vividly than in life, the fundamental reason why the suits, far from disguising the social class of those who wore them, underlined and emphasised it.

Their suits deform them. Wearing them, they look as though they were physically mis-shapen. A past style in clothes often looks absurd until it is re-incorporated into fashion. Indeed the economic logic of fashion depends on making the old-fashioned look absurd. But here we are not faced primarily with that kind of absurdity; here the clothes look less absurd, less 'abnormal' than the men's bodies which are in them.

The musicians give the impression of being unco-ordinated, bandy-legged, barrel-chested, low-arsed, twisted or scalene. The violinist on the right is made to look almost like a dwarf. None of their abnormalities is extreme. They do not provoke pity. They are just sufficient to undermine physical dignity. We look at bodies which appear coarse, clumsy, brute-like. And incorrigibly so.

Now make the experiment the other way round. Cover the bodies of the band and look only at their faces. They are country faces. Nobody could suppose that they are a group of barristers or managing directors. They are five men from a village who like to make music and do so with a certain self-respect. As we look at the faces we can imagine what the bodies would look like. And what we imagine is quite different from what we have just seen. In imagination we see them as their parents might remember them when absent. We accord them the normal dignity they have.

To make the point clearer, let us now consider an image when tailored clothes, instead of deforming, *preserve* the physical identity and therefore the natural authority of those wearing them. I have deliberately chosen a Sander photograph which looks old-fashioned and could easily lend itself to parody: the photograph of four Protestant missionaries in 1931.

Despite the portentousness, it is not even necessary to make the experiment of blocking out the faces. It is clear that here the suits actually confirm and enhance the physical presence of those wearing them. The clothes convey the same message as the faces and as the history of the bodies they hide. Suits, experience, social formation and function coincide.

Look back now at the three on the road to the dance. Their hands look too big, their bodies too thin, their legs too short. (They use their walking sticks as though they were driving cattle.) We can make the same experiment with the faces and the effect is exactly the same as with the band. They can wear only their hats as if they suited them.

Where does this lead us? Simply to the conclusion that peasants can't buy good suits and don't know how to wear them? No, what is at issue here is a graphic, if small, example (perhaps one of the most graphic which exists) of what Gramsci called class hegemony. Let us look at the contradictions involved more closely.

Most peasants, if not suffering from malnutrition, are physically strong and well-developed. Well-developed because of the very varied hard physical work they do. It would be too simple to make a list of physical characteristics – broad hands through working with them from a very early age, broad shoulders relative to the body through the habit of carrying, and so on. In fact many variations and exceptions also exist. One can, however, speak of a characteristic physical rhythm which most peasants, both women and men, acquire.

This rhythm is directly related to the energy demanded by the amount of work which has to be done in a day, and is reflected in typical physical movements and stance. It is an extended sweeping rhythm. Not necessarily slow. The traditional acts of scything or sawing may exemplify it. The way peasants ride horses makes it distinctive, as also the way they walk, as if testing the earth with each stride. In addition peasants possess a special physical dignity: this is determined by a kind of functionalism, a way of being *fully at home in effort.*

The suit, as we know it today, developed in Europe as a professional ruling-class costume in the last third of the 19th century. Almost anonymous as a uniform, it was the first ruling-class costume to idealise purely *sedentary* power. The power of the administrator and conference table. Essentially the suit was made for the gestures of talking and calculating abstractly. (As distinct, compared to previous upper-class costumes, from the gestures of riding, hunting, dancing, duelling.)

It was the English *gentleman*, with all the apparent restraint which that new stereotype implied, who launched the suit. It was a costume which inhibited vigorous action, and which action ruffled, uncreased and spoilt. 'Horses sweat, men perspire and women glow.' By the turn of the century, and increasingly after the first world war, the suit was mass-produced for mass urban and rural markets.

The physical contradiction is obvious. Bodies which are fully at home in effort, bodies which are used to extended sweeping movement: clothes idealising the sedentary, the discrete, the effortless. I would be the last to argue for a return to traditional peasant costumes. Any such return is bound to be escapist, for these costumes were a form of capital handed down through generations, and in the world today, in which every corner is dominated by the market, such a principle is anachronistic.

We can note, however, how traditional peasant working or ceremonial clothes respected the specific character of the bodies they were clothing. They were in general loose, and only tight in places where they were gathered to allow for freer movement. They were the antithesis of tailored clothes, clothes cut to follow the idealised shape of a more or less stationary body and then to hang from it!

Yet nobody forced peasants to buy suits, and the three on their way to the dance are clearly proud of them. They wear them with a kind of panache. This is exactly why the suit might become a classic and easily taught example of class hegemony.

Villagers – and, in a different way, city workers – were persuaded to choose suits. By publicity. By the new mass media. By salesmen. By example. By the sight of new kinds of travellers. And also by political developments of accommodation and state central organisation. For example: in 1900, on the occasion of the great Universal Exhibition, all the mayors of

France were, for the first time ever, invited to a banquet in Paris. Most of them were the peasant mayors of village communes. Nearly 30,000 came! And, naturally, for the occasion the vast majority wore suits.

The working classes – but peasants were simpler and more naïve about it than workers – came to accept as *their own* certain standards of the class that ruled over them – in this case standards of chic and sartorial worthiness. At the same time their very acceptance of these standards, their very conforming to these norms which had nothing to do with either their own inheritance or their daily experience, condemned them, within the system of those standards, to being always, and recognisably to the classes above them, second-rate, clumsy, uncouth, defensive. That indeed is to succumb to a cultural hegemony.

Perhaps one can nevertheless propose that when the three arrived and had drunk a beer or two, and had eyed the girls (whose clothes had not yet changed so drastically), they hung up their jackets, took off their ties, and danced, maybe wearing their hats, until the morning and the next day's work.

1979

The Eyes of Claude Monet

Too much has been made of Cézanne's famous remark that, if Monet was only an eye, what an eye! More important now, perhaps, to acknowledge and question the sadness in Monet's eyes, a sadness which emerges from photograph after photograph.

Little attention has been paid to this sadness because there is no place for it in the usual art-historical version of the meaning of Impressionism. Monet was the leader of the Impressionists – the most consistent and the most intransigent – and Impressionism was the beginning of Modernism, a kind of triumphal arch through which European art passed to enter the twentieth century.

There is some truth in this version. Impression-ism *did* mark a break with the previous history of European painting and a great deal of what followed – Post-Impressionism, Expressionism, Abstraction – can be thought of as being partly engendered by this first modern movement. It is equally true that today, after half a century, Monet's later works – and particularly the water lilies – appear now to have prefigured the work of artists such as Pollock, Tobey, Sam Francis, Rothko.

It is possible to argue, as Malevich did, that the twenty paintings which Monet made in the early 1890s of the façade of Rouen Cathedral, as seen at different times of day and under different weather conditions, were the final systematic proof that the history of painting would never be the same again. This history had henceforward to admit that every appearance could be thought of as a mutation and that visibility itself should be considered flux.

Furthermore, if one thinks of the claustrophobia of mid-nineteenth-century bourgeois culture, it is impossible not to see how Impressionism appeared as a liberation. To paint out of doors in front of the motif; to observe directly, to accord to light its proper hegemony in the domain of the visible; to relativize all colours (so that everything sparkles); to abandon the painting of dusty legends and all direct ideology; to speak of everyday appearances within the experience of a wide urban public (a day off, a trip to the country, boats, smiling women in sunlight, flags, trees in flower – the Impressionist vocabulary of images is that of a popular dream, the awaited, beloved, secular Sunday); the innocence of Impressionism – innocence in the sense that it did away with the secrets of painting, everything was there in the full light of day, there was nothing more to hide, and amateur painting followed easily – how could all this not be thought of as a liberation?

Why can't we forget the sadness in Monet's eyes, or simply acknowledge it as something personal to him, the result of his early poverty, the death of his first wife when so young, his failing eyesight when old? And in any case, are we not running the risk of explaining the history of Egypt as the consequence of Cleopatra's smile? Let us run the risk.

Twenty years before painting the façade of Rouen Cathedral, Monet painted (he was thirty-two years old) 'Impression Soleil Levant', and from this the critic Castagnary coined the term *Impressionist*. The painting is a view of the port of Le Havre where Monet was brought up as a child. In the foreground is the tiny silhouette of a man standing and rowing with another figure in a dinghy. Across the water, masts and derricks are dimly visible in the morning twilight. Above, but low in the sky, is a small orange sun and, below, its inflamed reflection in the water. It is not an image of dawn (Aurora), but of a day slipping in, as yesterday slipped out. The mood is reminiscent of Baudelaire's 'Le Crépuscule de Matin', in which the coming day is compared to the sobbing of somebody who has just been woken.

Yet what is it that exactly constitutes the melancholy of this painting? Why, for example, don't comparable scenes, as painted by Turner, evoke a similar mood? The answer is the painting method, precisely that practice which was to be called Impressionist. The transparency of the thin pigment representing the water – the thread of the canvas showing through it, the swift broken-straw-like brush strokes suggesting ripples of spars, the scrubbed-in areas of shadow, the reflections staining the water, the optical truthfulness and the *objective* vagueness, all this renders the scene makeshift, threadbare, decrepit. It is an image of homelessness. Its very insubstantiality makes shelter in it impossible. Looking at it, the idea occurs to you of a man trying to find his road home through a theatre décor. Baudelaire's lines in 'La Cygne', published in 1860, belong to the slow intake of breath before the accuracy and the refusal of this scene.

> . . . La forme d'une ville
> Change plus vite, hélas, que le coeur d'un
> mortel.

If Impressionism was about 'impressions', what change did this imply in the relation between seen and seer? (Seer here meaning both painter and viewer.) You do not have an *impression* of a scene with which you feel yourself to be longstandingly familiar. An impression is more or less fleeting; it is what is *left behind* because the scene has disappeared or changed. Knowledge can coexist with the known; and impression, by contrast, survives alone. However intensely and empirically observed at the moment, an impression later becomes, like a memory, impossible to verify. (Throughout his life Monet complained, in letter after letter, about not being able to complete a painting already begun, because the weather and therefore the subject, the motif, had irredeemably changed.) The new relation between scene and seer was such that now the scene was more fugitive, more chimerical than the seer. And there we find ourselves returned to the same lines by Baudelaire: 'La forme d'une ville . . .'

Suppose we examine the experience offered by a more typical Impressionist painting. In the spring of the same year as 'Le Soleil Levant' (1872) Monet painted two pictures of a lilac tree in his garden at Argenteuil. One shows the tree on a cloudy day and the other on a sunny day. Lying on the lawn beneath the tree in both pictures are three barely distinguishable figures. (They are thought to be Camille, Monet's first wife, Sisley and Sisley's wife.)

In the overcast picture these figures resemble moths in the lilac shade; in the second, dappled with sunlight, they become almost as invisible as lizards. (What betrays their presence is in fact the viewer's past experience; somehow the viewer distinguishes the mark of a profile with a tiny ear from the other almost identical marks which are only leaves.)

In the overcast picture the flowers of the lilac glow like mauve copper; in the second picture the whole scene is alight, like a newly lit fire: both are animated by a different kind of light energy, there is apparently no longer a trace of decrepitude, everything radiates. Purely optically? Monet would have nodded his head. He was a man of few words. Yet it goes much further.

Before the painted lilac tree you experience something unlike anything felt in front of any earlier painting. The difference is not a question of new optical elements, but of a new relation between what you are seeing and what you have seen. Every spectator can recognize this after a moment's introspection; all that may differ is the personal choice of which paintings reveal the new relation most vividly. There are hundreds of Impressionist paintings, painted during the 1870s, to choose from.

The painted lilac tree is both more precise and more vague than any painting you have seen before. Everything has been more or less sacrificed to the optical precision of its colours and tones. Space, measurement, action (history), identity, all are submerged within the play of light. One must remember here that *painted* light, unlike the real thing, is *not* transparent. The painted light covers, buries, the painted objects, a little like snow covering a landscape. (And the attraction of snow to Monet, the attraction of things being lost without a loss of first degree reality, probably corresponded to a deep psychological need.) So the new energy *is* optical? Monet was right to nod his head? The painted light dominates everything? No, because all this ignores how the painting actually works on the viewer.

Given the precision and the vagueness, you are forced to re-see the lilacs of your own experience. The precision triggers your visual memory, while the vagueness welcomes and accommodates your memory when it comes. More than that, the uncovered memory of your sense of sight is so acutely evoked, that other appropriate memories of other senses – scent, warmth, dampness, the texture of a dress, the length of an afternoon – are also extracted from the past. (One cannot help but think again of Baudelaire's *Correspondances*.) You fall through a kind of whirlpool of sense memories towards an ever receding moment of pleasure, which is a moment of total recognition.

The intensity of this experience can be

hallucinating. The fall into and towards the past with its mounting excitement, which, at the same time, is the mirror-opposite of expectation for it is a return, a withdrawal, has something about it which is comparable with an orgasm. Finally everything is simultaneous with and indivisible from the mauve fire of the lilac.

And all this follows – surprisingly – from Monet's affirmation, with slightly different words on several occasions, that 'the motif is for me altogether secondary; what I want to represent is what exists between the motif and me' (1895). What *he* had in mind were colours; what is bound to come into the viewer's mind are memories. If, in a generalized way, Impressionism lends itself to nostalgia (obviously in particular cases the intensity of the memories precludes nostalgia) it is not because we are living a century later, but simply because of the way the paintings always demanded to be read.

What then has changed? Previously the viewer entered into a painting. The frame or its edges were a threshold. A painting created its own time and space which were like an alcove to the world, and their experience, made clearer than it usually is in life, endured changeless and could be visited. This had little to do with the use of any systematic perspective. It is equally true, say, of a Sung Chinese landscape. It is more a question of permanence than space. Even when the scene depicted was momentary – for example, Caravaggio's 'Crucifixion of St Peter' – the momentariness is held within a continuity: the arduous pulling up of the cross constitutes part of the permanent assembly point of the painting. Viewers passed one another in Pierro della Francesca's 'Tent of Solomon' or on Grünewald's 'Golgotha' or in the bedroom of Rembrandt. But not in Monet's 'Gare de St Lazare'.

Impressionism closed that time and that space. What an Impressionist painting shows is painted in such a way that *you are compelled to recognize that it is no longer there.* It is here and here only that Impressionism is close to photography. You cannot enter an Impressionist painting; instead it extracts your memories. In a sense it is more active than you – the passive viewer is being born; what you receive is taken from what happens *between* you and it. No more within it. The memories extracted are often pleasurable – sunlight, river banks, poppy fields – yet they are also anguished, because each viewer remains alone. The viewers are as separate as the brush strokes. There is no longer a common meeting place.

Let us now return to the sadness in Monet's eyes. Monet believed that his art was forward-looking and based on a scientific study of nature. Or at least this is what he began by believing and never renounced. The degree of sublimation involved in such a belief is poignantly demonstrated by the story of the painting he made of Camille on her death bed. She died in 1879, aged thirty-two. Many years later Monet confessed to his friend Clemenceau that his need to analyse colours was both the joy and torment of his life. To the point where, he went on to say, I one day found myself looking at my beloved wife's dead face and just systematically noting the colours, according to an automatic reflex!

Without doubt the confession was sincere, yet the evidence of the painting is quite otherwise. A blizzard of white, grey, purplish paint blows across the pillows of the bed, a terrible blizzard of loss which will for ever efface her features. In fact there can be very few death-bed paintings which have been so intensely felt or subjectively expressive.

And yet to this – the consequence of his own act of painting – Monet was apparently blind. The positivistic and scientific claims he made for his art never accorded with its true nature. The same was equally true of his friend Zola. Zola believed that his novels were as objective as laboratory reports. Their real power (as is so evident in *Germinal*) comes from deep – and dark – unconscious feeling. At this period the mantle of progressive positivist enquiry some-times hid the very same premonition of loss, the same fears, of which, earlier, Baudelaire had been the prophet.

And this explains why *memory* is the unacknow-ledged axis of all Monet's work. His famous love of the sea (in which he wanted to be buried when he died), of rivers, of water, was perhaps a symbolic way of speaking of tides, sources, recurrence.

In 1896 he returned to paint again one of the cliffs near Dieppe which he had painted on several occa-sions fourteen years earlier. ('Falaise à Vavengeville', 'Gorge du Petit-Ailly'.) The painting, like many of his works of the same period, is heavily worked, encrusted, and with the minimum of tonal con-trast. It reminds you of thick honey. Its concern is no longer the instantaneous scene, as revealed in the light, but rather the slower dissolution of the scene by the light, a development which led towards a more decorative art. Or at least this is the usual 'explanation' based on Monet's own premises.

It seems to me that this painting is about some-thing quite different. Monet worked on it, day after day, believing that he was interpreting the effect of sunlight as it dissolved every detail of grass and shrub into a cloth of honey hung by the sea. But he wasn't, and the painting has really very little to do with sunlight. What he himself was dissolving into the honey cloth were all his previous memories of that cliff, so that it should absorb and contain them all. It is this almost desperate wish to save *all* which makes it such an amorphous, flat (and yet, if one recognizes it for what it is, touching) image.

And something very similar is happening in Monet's paintings of the water lilies in his garden during the last period of his life (1900–1926) at Giverny. In these paintings, endlessly reworked in face of the optically impossible task of combining flowers, reflections, sunlight, underwater reeds, refractions, ripples, surface, depths, the real aim was neither decorative nor optical; it was to preserve everything essential about the garden, which he had made, and which now as an old man he loved more than anything else in the world. The painted lily pond was to be a pond that remembered all.

And here is the crux of the contradiction which Monet as a painter lived. Impressionism closed the time and space in which previously painting had been able to preserve experience. And, as a result of this closure, which of course paralleled and was finally determined by other developments in late-nineteenth-century society, both painter and viewer found themselves more alone than ever before, more ridden by the anxiety that their own experience was ephemeral and meaningless. Not even all the charm and beauty of the Île de France, a Sunday dream of paradise, was a consolation for this.

Only Cézanne understood what was happening. Single-handed, impatient, but sustained by a faith that none of the other Impressionists had, he set himself the monumental task of creating a new form of time and space within the painting, so that finally experience might again be shared.

1980

The Production of the World

I no longer know how many times I have arrived at the Central Station in Amsterdam, nor how many times I have been to the Rijksmuseum to look at Vermeer or Fabritius or Van Gogh. The first time must have been nearly thirty years ago, and during the last seven years I have been to Amsterdam systematically every six months to attend meetings of the Transnational Institute, of which I am a fellow.

I come away from each meeting where twenty or so fellows from the Third World, the United States, Latin America, Britain and the Continent discuss aspects of the world situation within a socialist perspective – I come away each time a little less ignorant and more determined. By now we all know each other well and when we reassemble it is like a team coming together; sometimes we win, sometimes we are beaten. Each time we find ourselves battling against false representations of the world – either those of ruling-class propaganda or those we carry within ourselves.

I owe this Institute a great deal, yet the last time I was due to go to Amsterdam I almost decided not to go. I felt too exhausted. My exhaustion, if I may so put it, was as much metaphysical as physical. I could no longer hold meanings together. The mere thought of making connections filled me with anguish. The only hope was to stay put. Nevertheless at the last minute I went.

It was a mistake. I could scarcely follow anything. The connection between words and what they signified had been broken. It seemed to me that I was lost; the first human power – the power to name – was failing, or had always been an illusion. All was dissolution. I tried joking, lying down, taking a cold shower, drinking coffee, not drinking coffee, talking to myself, imagining faraway places – none of it helped.

I left the building, crossed the street and entered the Van Gogh museum, not in order to look at the paintings but because I thought that the one person who could take me home might be there; she was, but before I found her I had to run the gauntlet of the paintings. At this moment, I told myself, you need Van Gogh like you need a hole in the head.

'It seems to me not impossible that cholera, gravel, consumption may be celestial means of transport just as steamships, buses, railways, are means of transport on this earth. To die quietly of old age would be like going on foot . . .' Van Gogh wrote in a letter to his brother, Theo.

Still I found myself glancing at the paintings and then looking at them. 'The Potato Eaters'. 'The Cornfield with a Lark'. 'The Ploughed Field at Auvers'. 'The Pear Tree'. Within two minutes – and for the first time in three weeks – I was calm, reassured. Reality had been confirmed. The transformation was as quick and thorough-going as one of those sensational changes that can sometimes come about after an intravenous injection. And yet these paintings, already very familiar to me, had never before manifested anything like this therapeutic power.

What, if anything, does such a subjective experience reveal? What is the connection, if any, between my experience in the Van Gogh museum and the life work of Van Gogh the painter? I would have been tempted to reply: none or very little, were it not for a strange correspondence. Sometime after my return from Amsterdam I happened to take up a book of stories and essays by Hugo von Hofmannsthal. Among them is a story entitled 'Letters of a Traveller Come Home'. The 'letters' are dated 1901. The supposed letter-writer is a German businessman who has lived most of his life outside

Europe; now that he has returned to his homeland, he increasingly suffers from a sense of unreality; Europeans are not as he remembered them, their lives mean nothing because they systematically compromise.

'As I told you, I cannot grasp them, not by their faces, not by their gestures, not by their words; for their Being is no longer anywhere, indeed they *are* no longer anywhere.'

His disappointment leads him on to question his own memories and finally the credibility of anything. In many respects these thirty pages are a kind of prophecy of Sartre's *Nausea*, written thirty years later. This is from the last letter:

> Or again – some trees, those scraggy but well-kept trees which, here and there, have been left in the squares, emerging from the asphalt, protected by railings. I would look at them and I would know that they reminded me of trees – and yet were not trees – and then a shudder, seizing me, would break my breast in two, as though it were the breath, the indescribable breath of everlasting nothingness, of the everlasting nowhere, something which comes, not from death, from non-being.

The final letter also relates how he had to attend a business meeting in Amsterdam. He was feeling spineless, lost, indecisive. On his way there he passed a small art gallery, paused, and decided to go inside.

> How am I to tell you half of what these paintings said to me? They were a total justification of my strange and yet profound feelings. Here suddenly I was in front of something, a mere glimpse of which had previously, in my state of torpor, been too much for me. I had been haunted by that glimpse. Now a total stranger was offering me – with incredible authority – a reply – an entire world in the form of a reply.

The ending of the story is unexpected. Rehabilitated, confirmed, he went on to his meeting and pulled off the best business coup of his entire career.

A PS to the final letter gives the name of the artist in question as being a certain Vincent Van Gogh.

What is the nature of this 'entire world' which Van Gogh offers 'in the form of a reply' to a particular kind of anguish?

For an animal its natural environment and habitat are a given; for a man – despite the faith of the empiricists – reality is not a given: it has to be continually sought out, held – I am tempted to say *salvaged.* We are taught to oppose the real to the imaginary, as though one were always at hand and the other distant, far away. And this opposition is false. Events are always to hand. But the coherence of these events – which is what we mean by reality – is an imaginative construction. Reality always *lies beyond*, and this is as true for materialists as for idealists, for Plato and for Marx. Reality, however one interprets it, lies beyond a screen of clichés. Every culture produces such a screen, partly to facilitate its own practices (to establish habits) and partly to consolidate its own power. Reality is inimical to those with power.

All modern artists have thought of their innovations as offering a closer approach to reality, as a way of making reality more evident. It is here, and only here, that the modern artist and the revolutionary have sometimes found themselves side by side, both inspired by the idea of pulling down the screen of clichés, clichés which in the modern period have become unprecedentedly trivial and egotistical.

Yet many such artists have reduced what they found beyond the screen, to suit their own talent and social position as artists. When this has happened they have justified themselves with one of the dozen variants of the theory of art for art's sake.

They say: reality is art. They hope to extract an artistic profit from reality. Of no one is this less true than Van Gogh.

We know from his letters how intensely he was aware of the screen. His whole life story is one of an endless yearning for reality. Colours, the Mediterranean climate, the sun were for him vehicles going towards this reality; they were never objects of longing in themselves. This yearning was intensified by the crises he suffered when he felt that he was failing to salvage any reality at all. Whether these crises are today diagnosed as being schizophrenic or epileptic changes nothing; their content, as distinct from their pathology, was a vision of reality consuming itself like a phoenix.

We also know from his letters that nothing appeared more sacred to him than work. He saw the physical reality of labour as being, simultaneously, a necessity, an injustice and the essence of humanity to date. The artist's creative act was for him only one among many. He believed that reality could best be approached through work, precisely because reality itself was a form of production.

The paintings speak of this more clearly than words. Their so-called clumsiness, the gestures with which he drew with pigment upon the canvas, the gestures (invisible to us but imaginable) with which he chose and mixed his colours on the palette, all the gestures with which he handled and manufactured the stuff of the painted image, are analogous to the *activity* of the existence of what he is painting. His paintings imitate the active existence – the labour of being – of what they depict.

Take a chair, a bed, a pair of boots. His act of painting them was far nearer than that of any other painter to the carpenter's or the shoemaker's act of making them. He brings together the elements of the product – legs, cross bars, back, seat; sole, uppers, tongue, heel – as though he too were fitting them together, *joining* them, and as if this *being joined* constituted their reality.

Before a landscape the process required was far more complicated and mysterious, yet it followed the same principle. If one imagines God creating the world from earth and water, from clay, his way of handling it to make a tree or a cornfield might well resemble the way that Van Gogh handled paint when he painted that tree or cornfield. I am not suggesting that there was something quasi-divine about Van Gogh: this would be to fall into the worst kind of hagiography. If, however, we think of the creation of the world, we can imagine the act only through the visual evidence, before our eyes here and now, of the energy of the forces in play. And to these energies, Van Gogh was terribly – and I choose the adverb carefully – attuned.

When he painted a small pear tree in flower, the act of the sap rising, of the bud forming, the bud breaking, the flower forming, the styles thrusting out, the stigmas becoming sticky, these acts were present for him in the act of painting. When he painted a road, the roadmakers were there in his imagination. When he painted the turned earth of a ploughed field, the gesture of the blade turning the earth was included in his own act. Wherever he looked he saw the labour of existence; and this labour, recognized as such, for him constituted reality.

If he painted his own face, he painted the construction of his destiny, past and future, rather as palmists believe they can read this construction in the hand. His contemporaries who considered him abnormal were not all as stupid as is now assumed. He painted compulsively – no other painter was ever compelled in a comparable way.

His compulsion? It was to bring the two acts of production, that of the canvas and that of the reality depicted, ever closer and closer. This compulsion derived not from an idea about art – this is why it never occurred to him to profit from reality – but from an overwhelming feeling of empathy.

'I admire the bull, the eagle, and man with such

an intense adoration, that it will certainly prevent me from ever becoming an ambitious person.'

He was compelled to go ever closer, to approach and approach and approach. *In extremis* he approaches so close that the stars in the night sky became maelstroms of light, the cypress trees ganglions of living wood responding to the energy of wind and sun. There are canvases where reality dissolves him, the painter. But in hundreds of others he takes us as close as any man can, while remaining intact, to that permanent process by which reality is being produced.

Once, long ago, paintings were compared with mirrors. Van Gogh's might be compared with lasers. They do not wait to receive, they go out to meet, and what they traverse is, not so much empty space, as the act of production. The 'entire world' that Van Gogh offers as a reply to the vertigo of nothingness is the production of the world. Painting after painting is a way of saying, with awe but little comfort: it works.

1983

Steps Towards a Small Theory of the Visible

When I say the first line of the Lord's Prayer: 'Our father who art in heaven . . .' I imagine this heaven as invisible, unenterable but intimately close. There is nothing baroque about it, no swirling infinite space or stunning foreshortening. To find it – if one had the grace – it would only be necessary to lift up something as small and as at hand as a pebble or a salt-cellar on the table. Perhaps Cellini knew this.

'Thy kingdom come . . .' The difference is infinite between heaven and earth, yet the distance is minimal. Simone Weil wrote concerning this sentence: 'Here our desire pierces through time to find eternity behind it and this happens when we know how to turn whatever happens, no matter what it is, into an object of desire.'

Her words might also be a prescription for the art of painting.

Today images abound everywhere. Never has so much been depicted and watched. We have glimpses at any moment of what things look like on the other side of the planet, or the other side of the moon: Appearances registered, and transmitted with lightning speed.

Yet with this, something has innocently changed. They used to be called *physical* appearances because they belonged to solid bodies. Now appearances are volatile. Technological innovation has made it easy to separate the apparent from the existent. And this is precisely what the present system's mythology continually needs to exploit. It turns appearances into refractions, like mirages: refractions not of light but of appetite, in fact a single appetite, the appetite for more.

Consequently – and oddly, considering the physical implications of the notion of *appetite* – the existent, the body, disappears. We live within a spectacle of empty clothes and unworn masks.

Consider any newsreader on any television channel in any country. These speakers are the mechanical epitome of the *disembodied*. It took the system many years to invent them and to teach them to talk as they do.

No bodies and no Necessity – for Necessity is the condition of the existent. It is what makes reality real. And the system's mythology requires only the not-yet-real, the virtual, the next purchase. This produces in the spectator, not, as claimed, a sense of freedom (the so-called freedom of choice) but a profound isolation.

Until recently, history, all the accounts people gave of their lives, all proverbs, fables, parables, confronted the same thing: the everlasting, fearsome, and occasionally beautiful, struggle of living with Necessity, which is the enigma of existence – that which followed from the Creation, and which subsequently has always continued to sharpen the human spirit. Necessity produces both tragedy and comedy. It is what you kiss or bang your head against.

Today, in the system's spectacle, it exists no more. Consequently no experience is communicated. All that is left to share is the spectacle, the game that nobody plays and everybody can watch. As has never happened before, people have to try to place their own existence and their own pains single-handed in the vast arena of time and the universe.

I had a dream in which I was a strange dealer: a dealer in looks or appearances. I collected and distributed them. In the dream I had just discovered a secret! I discovered it on my own, without help or advice.

The secret was to get inside whatever I was

looking at – a bucket of water, a cow, a city (like Toledo) seen from above, an oak tree, and, once inside, to arrange its appearances for the better. *Better* did not mean making the thing seem more beautiful or more harmonious; nor did it mean making it more typical, so that the oak tree might represent all oak trees; it simply meant making it more itself so that so that the cow or the city or the bucket of water became more evidently unique!

The *doing* of this gave me pleasure and I had the impression that the small changes I made from the inside gave pleasure to others.

The secret of how to get inside the object so as to rearrange how it looked was as simple as opening the door of a wardrobe. Perhaps it was merely a question of being there when the door swung open on its own. Yet when I woke up, I couldn't remember how it was done and I no longer knew how to get inside things.

The history of painting is often presented as a history of succeeding styles. In our time art dealers and promoters have used this battle of styles to make brand-names for the market. Many collectors – and museums – buy names rather than works.

Maybe it's time to ask a naive question: what does all painting from the Palaeolithic period until our century have in common? Every painted image announces: *I have seen this*, or, when the making of the image was incorporated into a tribal ritual: *We have seen this*. The *this* refers to the sight represented. Non-figurative art is no exception. A late canvas by Rothko represents an illumination or a coloured glow which derived from the painter's experience of the visible. When he was working, he judged his canvas according to something else that he *saw*.

Painting is, first, an affirmation of the visible which surrounds us and which continually appears and disappears. Without the disappearing, there would perhaps be no impulse to paint, for then the visible itself would possess the surety (the permanence) which painting strives to find. More directly than any other art, painting is an affirmation of the existent, of the physical world into which mankind has been thrown.

Animals were the first subject in painting. And right from the beginning and then continuing through Sumerian, Assyrian, Egyptian and early Greek art, the depiction of these animals was extraordinarily true. Many millennia had to pass before an equivalent 'life-likeness' was achieved in the depiction of the human body. At the beginning, the existent was what confronted man.

The first painters were hunters whose lives, like

everybody else's in the tribe, depended upon their close knowledge of animals. Yet the act of painting was not the same as the act of hunting: the relation between the two was magical.

In a number of early cave paintings there are stencil representations of the human hand beside the animals. We do not know what precise ritual this served. We do know that painting was used to confirm a magical 'companionship' between prey and hunter, or, to put it more abstractly, between the existent and human ingenuity. Painting was the means of making this companionship explicit and therefore (hopefully) permanent.

This may still be worth thinking about, long after painting has lost its herds of animals and its ritual function. I believe it tells us something about the nature of the act.

The impulse to paint comes neither from observation nor from the soul (which is probably blind) but from an encounter: the encounter between painter and model – even if the model is a mountain or a shelf of empty medicine bottles. Mont St Victoire as seen from Aix (seen from elsewhere it has a very different shape) was Cézanne's companion.

When a painting is lifeless it is the result of the painter not having the nerve to get close enough for a collaboration to start. He stays at a *copying* distance. Or, as in mannerist periods like today, he stays at an art-historical distance, playing stylistic tricks which the model knows nothing about.

To go in close means forgetting convention, reputation, reasoning, hierarchies and self. It also means risking incoherence, even madness. For it can happen that one gets too close and then the collaboration breaks down and the painter dissolves into the model. Or the animal devours or tramples the painter into the ground.

Every authentic painting demonstrates a collaboration. Look at Petrus Christus' portrait of a young girl in the Staatliche Museum of Berlin, or the stormy seascape in the Louvre by Courbet, or the mouse with an aubergine painted by Tchou-Ta in the seventeenth century, and it is impossible to deny the participation of the model. Indeed, the paintings are *not* first and foremost about a young woman, a rough sea or a mouse with a vegetable; they are about this participation. 'The brush,' wrote Shitao, the great seventeenth-century Chinese landscape painter, 'is for saving things from chaos.'

It is a strange area into which we are wandering and I'm using words strangely. A rough sea on the northern coast of France, one autumn day in 1870, *participating in being seen* by a man with a beard who, the following year, will be put in prison! Yet there is no other way of getting close to the actual practice of this silent art, which stops everything moving.

The *raison d'être* of the visible is the eye; the eye evolved and developed where there was enough light for the visible forms of life to become more and more complex and varied. Wild flowers, for example, are the colours they are in order to be seen. That an empty sky appears blue is due to the structure of our eyes and the nature of the solar system. There is a certain ontological basis for the collaboration between model and painter. Silesius, a seventeenth-century doctor of medicine in Wrocklau, wrote about the interdependence of the seen and the seeing in a mystical way:

> *La rose qui contemple ton oeil de chair*
> *A fleuri de la sorte en Dieu dans l'éternel*

How did you become what you visibly are? asks the painter.

I am as I am. I'm waiting, replies the mountain or the mouse or the child.

What for?

For you, if you abandon everything else.

For how long?

For as long as it takes.

There are other things in life.

Find them and be more normal.

And if I don't?

I'll give you what I've given nobody else, but it's worthless, it's simply the answer to your useless question.

Useless?

I am as I am.

No promise more than that?

None. I can wait for ever.

I'd like a normal life.

Live it and don't count on me.

And if I do count on you?

Forget everything and in me you'll find – me!

The collaboration which sometimes follows is seldom based on good will: more usually on desire, rage, fear, pity or longing. The modern illusion concerning painting (which post-modernism has done nothing to correct) is that the artist is a creator. Rather he is a receiver. What seems like creation is the act of giving form to what he has received.

Bogena and Robert and his brother Witek came to spend the evening because it was the Russian new year. Sitting at the table whilst they spoke Russian, I tried to draw Bogena. Not for the first time. I always fail because her face is very mobile and I can't forget her beauty. And to draw well you have to forget that. It was long past midnight when they left. As I was doing my last drawing, Robert said: This is your last chance tonight, just draw her, John, draw her and be a man!

When they had gone, I took the least bad drawing and started working on it with colours – acrylic. Suddenly, like a weather vane swinging round because the wind has changed, the portrait began to look like something. Her 'likeness' now was in my head – and all I had to do was to draw it out, not look for it. The paper tore. I rubbed on paint sometimes as thick as ointment. At four in the morning the face began to lend itself to, to smile at, its own representation.

The next day the frail piece of paper, heavy with paint, still looked good. In the daylight there were a few nuances of tone to change. Colours applied at night sometimes tend to be too desperate – like shoes pulled off without being untied. Now it was finished.

From time to time during the day I went to look at it and I felt elated. Because I had done a small drawing I was pleased with? Scarcely. The elation came from something else. It came from the face's *appearing* – as if out of the dark. It came from the fact that Bogena's face had made a present of *what it could leave behind of itself.*

★

What is a likeness? When a person dies, they leave behind, for those who knew them, an emptiness, a space: the space has contours and is different for each person mourned. This space with its contours is the person's *likeness* and is what the artist searches for when making a living portrait. A likeness is something left behind invisibly.

Soutine was among the great painters of the twentieth century. It has taken fifty years for this to become clear, because his art was both traditional and uncouth, and this mixture offended all fashionable tastes. It was as if his painting had a heavy broken accent and so was considered inarticulate: at best exotic, and at worst barbarian. Now his devotion to the existent becomes more and more exemplary. Few other painters have revealed more graphically than he the collaboration, implicit in the act of painting, between model and painter. The poplars, the carcasses, the children's faces on Soutine's canvases clung to his brush.

Shitao – to quote him again – wrote:

> Painting is the result of the receptivity of ink: the ink is open to the brush: the brush is open to the hand: the hand is open to the heart: all this in the same way as the sky engenders

what the earth produces: everything is the result of receptivity.

It is usually said about the late work of Titian or Rembrandt or Turner that their handling of paint became *freer*. Although, in a sense, true, this may give a false impression of *wilfulness*. In fact these painters in their old age simply became more receptive, more open to the appeal of the 'model' and its strange energy. It is as if their own bodies fall away.

When once the principle of collaboration has been understood, it becomes a criterion for judging works of any style, irrespective of their freedom of handling. Or rather (because *judgement* has little to do with art) it offers us an insight for seeing more clearly why painting moves us.

Rubens painted his beloved Hélène Fourment many times. Sometimes she collaborated, sometimes not. When she didn't, she remains a painted ideal; when she did, we too wait for her. There is a painting of roses in a vase by Morandi (1949) in which the flowers wait like cats to be let into his vision. (This is very rare for most flower paintings remain pure spectacle.) There is a portrait of a man painted on wood two millennia ago, whose participation we still feel. There are dwarfs painted by

Velázquez, dogs by Titian, houses by Vermeer in which we recognise, as energy, the will-to-be-seen.

More and more people go to museums to look at paintings and do not come away disappointed. What fascinates them? To answer: Art, or the history of art, or art appreciation, misses, I believe, the essential.

In art museums we come upon the visible of other periods and it offers us company. We feel less alone in face of what we ourselves see each day appearing and disappearing. So much continues to look the same: teeth, hands, the sun, women's legs, fish . . . in the realm of the visible all epochs coexist and are fraternal, whether separated by centuries or millennia. And when the painted image is not a copy but the result of a dialogue, the painted thing speaks if we listen.

In matters of seeing Joseph Beuys was the great prophet of the second half of our century, and his life's work was a demonstration of, and an appeal for, the kind of collaboration I'm talking about. Believing that everybody is potentially an artist, he took objects and arranged them in such a way that they beg the spectator to collaborate with them, not this time by painting, but by listening to what their eyes tell them and remembering.

★

I know of few things more sad (sad, not tragic) than an animal who has lost its sight. Unlike humans, the animal has no supporting language left which can describe the world. If on a familiar terrain, the blind animal manages to find its way about with its nose. But it has been deprived of the existent and with this deprivation it begins to diminish until it does little but sleep, therein perhaps hunting for a dream of that which once existed.

The Marquise de Sorcy de Thélusson, painted in 1790 by David, looks at me. Who could have foreseen in her time the solitude in which people today live? A solitude confirmed daily by networks of bodiless and false images concerning the world. Yet their falseness is not an error. If the pursuit of profit is considered as the only means of salvation for mankind, turnover becomes the absolute priority, and, consequently, the existent has to be disregarded or ignored or suppressed.

Today, to try to paint the existent is an act of resistance instigating hope.

I Would Softly Tell My Love

JANUARY 2002

FRIDAY

Nazim, I'm in mourning and I want to share it with you, as you shared so many hopes and so many mournings with us.

'The telegram came at night,
only three syllables:
"He is dead".'[1]

I'm mourning my friend Juan Muñoz, a wonderful artist, who makes sculptures and installation and who died yesterday on a beach in Spain, aged Forty-eight.

I want to ask you about something which puzzles me. After a natural death, as distinct from victimization, killing or dying from hunger, there is first the shock, unless the person has been ailing for a long while, then there is the monstrous sense of loss, particularly when the person is young –

'The day is breaking
but my room
is composed of a long night.'[2]

and there follows the pain, which says of itself that it will never end. Yet with this pain there comes, surreptitiously, something else which approaches a joke but is not one. (Juan was a good joker.) Something which hallucinates, a little similar to the gesture of a conjuror's handkerchief after a trick, a kind of lightness, totally opposed to what one is feeling. You recognize what I mean? Is this lightness a frivolity or a new instruction?

Five minutes after my asking you this, I received a fax from my son Yves, with some lines he had just written for Juan:

'You always appeared
        with a laugh
and a new trick.

You always disappeared
        leaving your hands
on our table.

You disappeared
          leaving your cards
in our hands.

You will re-appear
          with a new laugh
which will be a trick.'

SATURDAY

I'm not sure whether I ever saw Nazim Hikmet. I would swear to it that I did, but I can't find the circumstantial evidence. I believe it was in London in 1954. Four years after he had been released from prison, nine years before his death. He was speaking at a political meeting held in Red Lion Square. He said a few words and then he read some poems. Some in English, others in Turkish. His voice was strong, calm, highly personal and very musical. But it did not seem to come from his throat – or not from his throat at that moment. It was as though he had a radio in his breast, which he switched on and off with one of his large, slightly trembling, hands. I'm describing it badly because his presence and sincerity were very obvious. In one of his long poems he describes six people in Turkey listening in the early 1940s to a symphony by Shostakovich on the radio.

Three of the six people are (like him) in prison. The broadcast is live; the symphony is being played at that same moment in Moscow, several thousand kilometres away. Hearing him read his poems in Red Lion Square, I had the impression that the words he was saying were also coming from the other side of the world. Not because they were difficult to understand (they were not), nor because they were blurred or weary (they were full of the capacity of endurance), but because they were being said to somehow triumph over distances and to transcend endless separations. The *here* of all his poems is elsewhere.

'In Prague a cart –

a one-horse wagon
passes the Old Jewish Cemetery.
The cart is full of longing for another city,
I am the driver.'[3]

Even when he was sitting on the platform before he got up to speak, you could see he was an unusually large and tall man. It was not for nothing that he was nicknamed 'The tree with blue eyes'. When he did stand up, you had the impression he was also very light, so light that he risked to become airborne.

Perhaps I never did see him, for it would seem unlikely that, at a meeting organized in London by the international Peace movement, Hikmet would have been tethered to the platform by several guy-ropes so that he should remain earthbound. Yet that is my clear memory. His words after he pronounced them rose into the sky – it was a meeting outdoors – and his body made as if to follow the words he had written, as they drifted higher and higher above the Square and above the sparks of the one-time trams which had been suppressed three or four years before along Theobald's Road.

> 'You're a mountain village
>   in Anatolia,
>   you're my city,
>   most beautiful and most unhappy.
> You're a cry for help – I mean, you're my country;
>   the footsteps running towards you are mine.'[4]

MONDAY MORNING

Nearly all the contemporary poets who have counted most for me during my long life I have read in translation, seldom in their original language. I think it would have been impossible for anyone to say this before the twentieth century. Arguments about poetry being or not being translatable went on for centuries – but they were chamber arguments – like chamber music. During the twentieth century most of the chambers were reduced to rubble. New means of communication, global politics, imperialisms, world markets, etc. threw millions of people together and took millions of people apart in an indiscriminate and quite unprecedented way. And as a result the expectations of poetry changed; more and more the best poetry counted on readers who were further and further away.

> 'Our poems
> like milestones
> must line the road.'[5]

During the twentieth century, many naked lines of poetry were strung between different continents, between forsaken villages and distant capitals. You all know it, all of you; Hikmet, Brecht, Vallejo, Atilla Jósef, Adonis, Juan Gelman . . .

MONDAY AFTERNOON

When I first read some poems by Nazim Hikmet I was in my late teens. They were published in an obscure international literary review in London, which was published under the aegis of the British Communist Party. I was a regular reader. The Party line on poetry was crap, but the poems and stories published were often inspiring.

By that time, Meyerhold had already been executed in Moscow. If I think particularly now of Meyerhold, it is because Hikmet admired him, and was much influenced by him when he first visited Moscow in the early 1920s . . .

'I owe very much to the theatre of Meyerhold. In 1925 I was back in Turkey and I organized the first Worker's Theatre in one of the industrial districts of Istanbul. Working in this theatre as director and writer, I felt that it was Meyerhold who had opened to us new possibilities of working for and with the audience.'

After 1937, those new possibilities had cost Meyerhold his life, but in London readers of the Review did not yet know this.

What struck me about Hikmet's poems when I first discovered them was their space; they contained more space than any poetry I had until then read. They didn't describe space; they came through it, they crossed mountains. They were also about action. They related doubts, solitude, bereavement, sadness, but these feelings followed actions rather than being a substitute for action. Space and actions go together. Their antithesis is prison, and it was in Turkish prisons that Hikmet, as a political prisoner, wrote half his life's work.

WEDNESDAY

Nazim, I want to describe to you the table on which I'm writing. A white metal garden table, such as one might come across today in the grounds of a *yali* on the Bosphorus. This one is on the covered verandah of a small house in a southeast Paris suburb. This house was built in 1938, one of many houses built here at that time for artisans, tradesmen, skilled workers. In 1938 you were in prison. A watch was hanging on a nail above your bed. In the ward above yours three bandits in chains were awaiting their death sentence.

There are always too many papers on this table. Each morning the first thing I do, whilst sipping coffee, is to try to put them back into order. To the right of me there is a plant in a pot, which I know you would like. It has very dark leaves. Their undersurface is the colour of damsons; on top the light has *stained* them dark brown. The leaves are grouped in threes, as if they were night butterflies – and they are the same size as butterflies – feeding from the same flower. The plant's own flowers are very small, pink and as inno- cent as the voices of kids learning a song in a primary school. It's a kind of giant clover. This particular one came from Poland, where the plant's name is

Koniczyna. It was given to me by the mother of a friend who grew it in her garden near the Ukrainian border. She has striking blue eyes and can't stop touching her plants as she walks through the garden or moves around her house, just as some grandmothers can't stop touching their young grandchildren's heads.

> 'My love, my rose,
> my journey across the Polish plain has begun:
> I'm a small boy happy and amazed
> a small boy
> looking at his first picture book
>   of people
>   animals
>   objects, plants.'[6]

In story-telling everything depends upon what follows what. And the truest order is seldom obvious. Trial and error. Often many times. This is why a pair of scissors and a reel of scotch tape are also on the table. The tape is not fitted into one of those gadgets which makes it easy to tear off a length. I have to cut the tape with the scissors. What is hard is finding where the tape ends on the roll, and then unrolling it. I search impatiently, irritably with my fingernails. Consequently, when once I do find the end, I stick it on to the edge of the table, and I let the tape unroll until it touches the floor, then I leave it hanging there.

At times I walk out of the verandah into the adjoining room where I chat or eat or read a newspaper. A few days ago, I was sitting in this room and something caught my eye because it was moving. A minute cascade of twinkling water was falling, rippling, towards the verandah floor near the legs of my empty chair in front of the table. Streams in the Alps begin with no more than a trickle like this.

A reel of scotch tape stirred by a draught from a window is sometimes enough to move mountains.

THURSDAY EVENING

Ten years ago I was standing in front of a building in Istanbul near the Haydar-Pacha Station, where suspects were interrogated by the police. Political prisoners were held and cross-examined, sometimes for weeks, on the top floor. Hikmet was cross-examined there in 1938.

The building was not planned as a jail but as a massive administrative fortress. It appears indestructible and is built of bricks and silence. Prisons, constructed as such, have a sinister, but often, also, a nervous, makeshift air about them. For example, the prison in Bursa where Hikmet spent ten years was nicknamed 'the stone aeroplane', because of its irregular layout. The staid fortress I was looking at by the station in Istanbul had by contrast the confidence and tranquility of a monument to silence.

Whoever is inside here and whatever happens inside here – the building announced in measured tones – will be forgotten, removed from the record, buried in a crevice between Europe and Asia.

It was then that I understood something about his poetry's unique and inevitable strategy: it had to continually overreach its own confinement! Prisoners everywhere have always dreamt of the Great Escape, but Hikmet's poetry did not. His poetry, before it began, placed the prison as a small dot on the map of the world.

> 'The most beautiful sea
>> hasn't been crossed yet.
> The most beautiful child
>> hasn't grown up yet.
> Our most beautiful days
>> we haven't seen yet.
> And the most beautiful words I wanted to tell you
>> I haven't said yet.
>
> They've taken us prisoner,
> they've locked us up:
>> me inside the walls,
>>> you outside.

But that's nothing.
The worst
is when people – knowingly or not –
carry prison inside themselves . . .
Most people have been forced to do this,
honest, hard-working, good people
who deserve to be loved as much as I love you. [7]

His poetry, like a geometry compass, traced circles, sometimes intimate, sometimes wide and global, with only its sharp point inserted in the prison cell.

FRIDAY MORNING

Once I was waiting for Juan Muñoz in a hotel in Madrid, and he was late because, as I explained, when he was working hard at night he was like a mechanic under a car, and he forgot about time. When he eventually turned up, I teased him about lying on his back under cars. And later he sent me a joke fax which I want to quote to you, Nazim. I'm not sure why. Maybe the why isn't my business. I'm simply acting as a postman between two dead men.

'I would like to introduce myself to you – I am a Spanish mechanic (cars only, not motorcycles) who spends most of his time lying on his back underneath an engine looking for it! But – and this is the important issue – I make the occasional art work. Not that I am an artist. No. But I would like to stop this nonsense of crawling in and under greasy cars, and become the Keith Richard of the art world. And if this is not possible to work like the priests, half an hour only, and with wine.

'I'm writing to you because two friends (one in Porto and one in Rotterdam) want to invite you and me to the basement of the Boyman's Car Museum and to other cellars (hopefully more alcoholic) in the old town of Porto.

'They also mentioned something about landscape which I did not understand. Landscape! I think maybe it was something about driving and looking around, or looking around whilst driving around . . .

'Sorry Sir, another client just came in. Whoa! A Triumph Spitfire!'

I hear Juan's laughter, echoing in the studio where he is alone with his silent figures.

FRIDAY EVENING

Sometimes it seems to me that many of the greatest poems of the twentieth century – written by women as well as men – may be the most fraternal ever written. If so, this has nothing to do with political slogans. It applies to Rilke, who was apolitical; to

Borges, who was a reactionary; and to Hikmet, who was a life-long communist. Our century was one of unprecedented massacres, yet the future it imagined (and sometimes fought for) proposed fraternity. Very few earlier centuries made such a proposal.

'These men, Dino,
who hold tattered shreds of light
where are they going
in this gloom, Dino?
You, me too:
we are with them, Dino.
We too Dino
have glimpsed the blue sky.'[8]

SATURDAY

Maybe, Nazim, I'm not seeing you this time either. Yet I would swear to it that I am. You are sitting across the table from me on the verandah. Have you ever noticed how the shape of a head often suggests the mode of thinking which habitually goes on inside it? There are heads which relentlessly indicate speed of calculation. Others which reveal the determined pursuit of old ideas. Many these days betray the incomprehension of continuous loss. Your head – its size and your screwed-up blue eyes – suggests to me the coexistence of many worlds with different skies, one within another, inside it; not intimidating, calm, but used to overcrowding.

I want to ask you about the period we're living today. Much of what you believed was happening in history, or believed should happen, has turned out to be illusory. Socialism, as you imagined it, is being built nowhere. Corporate capitalism advances unimpeded – although increasingly contested – and the twin World Trade Towers have been blown up. The overcrowded world grows poorer every year. Where is the blue sky today that you saw with Dino?

Yes, those hopes, you reply, are in tatters, yet what does this really change? Justice is still a one-word prayer, as Ziggy Marley sings in your time now. The whole of history is about hopes being sustained, lost, renewed. And with new hopes come new theories. But for the overcrowded, for those who have little or nothing except, sometimes, courage and love, hope works differently. Hope is then something to bite on, to put between the teeth. Don't forget this. Be a realist. With hope between the teeth comes the strength to carry on even when fatigue never lets up, comes the strength, when necessary, to choose not to shout at the wrong moment, comes the strength above all not to howl. A person, with hope between her or his teeth, is a brother or sister who commands respect. Those without hope in the real world are condemned to be alone. The best they can offer is only pity. And whether these hopes between the teeth are fresh or tattered makes little difference when it comes to surviving the nights and imagining a new day. Do you have any coffee?

I'll make some.

I leave the verandah. When I come back from the kitchen with two cups – and the coffee is Turkish – you have left. On the table, very near where the scotch tape is stuck, there is a book, open at a poem you wrote in 1962.

> 'If I was a plane tree I would rest in its shade
> If I was a book
> I'd read without being bored on sleepless nights
> Pencil I would not want to be even between my
> > own fingers
> If I was door
> I would open for the good and shut for the wicked
> If I was window a wide open window without
> > curtains
> I would bring the city into my room
> If I was a word
> I'd call out for the beautiful the just the true
> If I was word
> I would softly tell my love.'[9]

2002

Notes

1. Nazim Hickmet, *The Moscow Symphony*. Trans. Taner Baybars. Rapp and Whiting Ltd, 1970.

2. Ibid.

3. Hickmet, *Prague Dawn*. Trans. Randy Blasing and Muten Konuk. Persea Books, 1994.

4. Hickmet, *You*. Trans. Blasing and Konuk. Ibid.

5. Trans. John Berger.

6. Hickmet, *Letter from Poland*. Trans. John Berger.

7. Hickmet, *9–10pm. Poems*. Trans. Blasing and Konuk.

8. Hickmet, *On a painting by Abidine entitled The Long March*. Trans. John Berger.

9. Hickmet, *Under the Rain*. Trans. Özen Ozüner and John Berger.